The Eight Step Strategy for Success in Real Estate Sales

And

The 18 Reasons Why Most New Real Estate Agents Fail

Featuring

The 13 Key Factors in Selecting a Real Estate Brokerage

1

This book is dedicated to my brilliant wife.

Her real estate success has led me to leave management consulting and join her in her real estate endeavors. Without her, this book would not be possible.

Motivation

This book will provide you with an understanding of what it takes to succeed in real estate sales.

Many people study for, pass their state's real estate exam, and receive their real estate licenses. They start their real estate careers, thinking great success will come quickly. It does not. They get disappointed. Some move from one brokerage to another, possibly again and again, assuming the grass is greener on the other side. Many give up and let their real estate licenses expire.

Multiple studies have shown that 80-90% of those who receive their licenses quit the business within one to two years. This does not need to happen to you.

This book is written for you if you are thinking about getting a real estate license but not sure. It is for you if you are studying for your real estate license, just received it, and want to start planning your next steps. It is also for you if you started in real estate in the past year or two and have still not found your path to success.

Overview

The book consists of an eight-step strategy for real estate success. It reflects the author's experiences in real estate sales, agent recruitment, and team management in his current career. The book also reflects his strategic and marketing planning expertise from his previous management consulting career.

Step 1 - Understanding the 18 reasons why most new real estate agents fail

Step 2 - Sharpening the relevant skills

Step 3 - Choosing your focus area

Step 4 - Selecting a brokerage to join

Step 5 - Defining your unique selling proposition

Step 6 - Defining your target market.

Step 7 - Marketing yourself, your brand, and your services to generate leads and convert to customers

Step 8 - Executing transactions to near perfection, allowing you to grow your reputation and client base through referrals and repeat business

Legal Disclaimer

Although the author and publisher made every effort to ensure that this book's information was accurate at press time, the author and publisher do not assume and hereby disclaim any liability to any party for any loss, damage, or disruption caused by errors or omissions.

The author and the publisher disclaim any and all liability to the maximum extent permitted by law if any information, analysis, opinions, advice, and/or recommendations in this book prove to be inaccurate, incomplete, unreliable, or result in any other losses.

The information contained in this book does not constitute legal or financial advice and should never be used without first consulting with legal and other professionals.

The publisher and the author do not make any guarantee or other promise as to any outcomes that may or may not be obtained from using this book's content. You should conduct your own research and due diligence.

Information in Step 8 is based on California specific real estate law and may or may not apply in your state. Laws and regulations referenced in this book are subject to change.

About the Author

David Gadish, Ph.D., is a tenured university professor, a former management consultant, licensed real estate professional, real estate trainer, and coach.

David is a founding partner at Geffen Real Estate in Beverly Hills, California, where he oversees a team of residential and commercial real estate agents.

David is a professor at the College of Business and Economics, California State University, Los Angeles. He also currently teaches real estate at Touro College Los Angeles, a division of Touro University Worldwide, where he established the current real estate program.

David is also the author of "The Eight Step Strategy for Success in Real Estate Sales: And The 18 Reasons Why Most New Real Estate Agents Fail, Featuring The 13 Key Factors in Selecting a Real Estate Brokerage".

In his spare time, David and his wife and business partner, Orit, raise their four daughters on their over 150 fruit tree orchard in Beverly Hills, California. David Gadish can be reached via text at 310-433-0694 or via email at david@GeffenRealEstate.com.

Brief Table of Contents

Table of Contents

Step 1 - Understanding Why Most New Real Estate Agents Fail

Lessons from the Many Agents that Have Failed Before, so You Don't Have to!

In my earlier years in real estate, while interviewing agents, I would hear each one of them with high expectations for themselves. They told themselves and me that they would do what it takes to create that success. Many would then walk into my office and announce that they were moving to a different brokerage, taking a break from real estate, or quitting altogether.

I would spend many hours mentoring each new agent, so I did not want to waste time with those that come and go. I thought that maybe it was me failing them somehow, so I would check up on them a few months and years later via the department of real estate search. I discovered that some just quit the business. Others flipped brokerages like flipping burgers at a fast-food chain, not finding their place. A few did succeed at different brokerages, and I am happy they found their fit.

I then started explaining to candidates, in great detail, both in writing and during the initial interview, how hard it is for most new agents to create success and why that was so.

I finally decided to put all of the reasons why most new agents don't make it as a starting point for this book.

Reason #1 - Thinking Money Will Come Quickly

Agents often ask, "how long before I start making money?" Or make statements like "I will give it a try for six months and see how it goes". The vast majority of agents do not close a deal quickly unless their mother or cousin, or friend has an immediate need or their broker assigns them a hot lead. For them, the first deal takes little effort.

And then what? They close that one deal. But when will the next one come? And the next one? And the next? Well, this requires effort and time.

New agents watch too many TV shows that showcase the glamorous lives of real estate agents. Many of these shows are staged productions and do not reflect reality.

Dealing with people is never easy, and especially so when it comes to vast sums of money...

Many clients believe agents make too much money, can be jealous of you even if you did not make it yet.

On many occasions, clients may treat agents as if it is ok for them to work for free and then switch agents, so you end up losing time and money. Owners of real estate often seek to list homes at unrealistically high prices, and when they do not sell, rather than reduce the price, they switch agents, believing that somehow it is their fault.

Buyers often believe they deserve to purchase properties well below list prices. Rather than increase their offers or seek lower-priced homes, they will tell you they need a break from their home search. A few weeks later, you discover that they ended up purchasing a home at a higher price than the upper limit they told you to search with a different agent.

Reason #3 - Personality Does Not Fit Real Estate Sales

To sell real estate, you need to excel in marketing. Would you enjoy marketing / promoting yourself, your brand, and your services again and again? Will you be able to accept rejection again and again and again? Will you enjoy negotiating again and again and again? Being nice but tough helps immensely in this business. Do you desire to be a real estate agent? Are you passionate about it?

Reason #4 - Not Having Sufficient Savings

Many new agents, possibly yourself, do not have bank accounts loaded with money that allows living for one or more years without making sufficient income from real estate alone.

You need money to live. You need money to pay your rent or mortgage, eat, and pay for all your other routine living expenses. You should be prepared for a worst-case scenario where you will not make money from real estate anytime soon. Can you survive 12-18 months before you start making money in real estate? Or, will you have to drop real estate after six months since you ran out of money to live?

Then there is the need for money for your business. While in most states will need to join a brokerage, you will be an independent contractor, and you will be starting your business. Some brokerages charge fees. All kinds of fees! We discuss these fees in Step 4. Other brokerages do not charge fees, which is nice. Either way, in most situations, you will need to pay to join a local association of realtors as well as a local multiple listing service (MLS). These cost money.

You will also need money for your marketing and business development efforts. While some brokerages may create marketing materials for you, they will doubtfully distribute thousands of flyers on your behalf at their own expense.

Reason #5 - Not Having A Sufficient Financial Support to Survive the Early Years

Many new agents do not have a mom, dad, husband, wife, or partner to help support them while they get started in real estate. If you do, this is great. It will allow you to take your time and build your business in a more stress-free environment. If you do not have such support or your own savings, read on.

Reason #6 - Not Having a Full or Part-Time Job to Survive the Early Years

Agents that do not have savings, financial support from their families, or a job are not likely to survive the initial period.

If you are in this situation, you should consider getting a part-time or a full-time job to pay your living and business expenses until you establish yourself and become profitable via real estate alone.

Reason #7 - Thinking that If They Start Part-Time Since They Have a Job, They can Start Slowly

It's great if you have a part-time job or a full-time job. Let this not stop you from starting in real estate sales, but be prepared to spend a substantial amount of time during evenings and weekends or whenever you are off from your job to dedicate to the pursuit of real estate sales.

Reason #8 - Not Dedicating Sufficient Time to Their Real Estate Business

There is no start or end time to real estate action. Real estate sales are conducted evenings and weekends as well as on weekdays.

You need to be accessible to your clients almost all the time. Having a job is fine if you are willing to reply to prospects and clients during your breaks and be ready to spend time before and after your working hours at that job.

And then there is marketing research, planning, and execution. These can be handled almost anytime.

Reason #9 - Not Having the Right Mentor

Agents that do have the financial ability to ride out the early years still fail since they often spin their wheels with no direction or guidance. It is critical to team up with the right mentor that you want to try to trust and let them guide you to success. Ensure that this mentor actually created their own success in real estate and is more than just a teacher teaching you theory.

Reason #10 - Lacking Focus, Specific Goals, a Strategic Plan, and a System to Implement It

The focus should be defined by your mentor and you in a collaborative effort based on who you are as a person, your background, interests, and desires. It should not be based on the interests of your mentor alone. It is ideal to have a match between your and your mentor's

interests clearly established before getting started at their brokerage.

Focus on your unique selling point (see Step 5). Focus on a specific target audience to market to (see Step 6).

Once you create a plan from these, with your broker's help, you need to systematically and consistently implement that plan.

Reason #11 - Changing Focus Again and Again and Again

Many agents that do start with a focus do not see immediate results. They then think that the current focus area will not work for them and decide to switch their focus. Some do so a few times and then quit the business.

It would help if you took the time to find the right focus area for you, and once you determine what it is with your broker's help, you should pursue it without giving up. It may take a few years before the business starts flowing at levels that allow you to dedicate all of your income-producing hours to real estate alone.

Many agents do not know where to find the people that could send them business. They also do not know how to convert them to clients.

Potential clients are everywhere, but you need to stay focused on a group of them and then pursue them repeatedly through sophisticated marketing campaigns.

You start with your existing network, grow it, and convert people to prospects and then to clients.

Reason #13 – Joining a Brokerage That Does Not Fit Their Personality

Many new agents join brokerages for all the wrong reasons. Some are looking for a fancy brand name, and some are looking for a large brokerage since they believe large means an opportunity to make more money.

It would help if you interviewed with different brokerages – national brands, regional brands, as well as boutique brokerages that focus on specific areas of real estate before you pick the brokerage that is best for you.

Reason #14 – Selecting A Focus Area That Does Not Fit Their Personality

Many agents start focusing on their mentor's focus area. That may not be the right fit for them.

You should survey the various focus areas (see Step 3) with your mentor and pick the one that best fits your personality and interests. You might also need to switch mentors if they do not provide you the level of support you need in your preferred focus area.

Reason #15 – Lacking Total Commitment

Many agents look at real estate sales as a business, a career, or a job. It is not. New agents need to look at real estate as an extension of their lives. They need to be surrounded by real estate like they need air to breathe and food to eat.

Many new agents are not willing to do whatever it takes within reason to achieve their goals, and so many of them fail.

Reason #16 - Giving Up Too Quickly

Some agents do not start making money within the first few months and stop believing in their own ability to create success. The first seven years or so since starting in real estate, my wife and I rented – first a one-bedroom and then a two-bedroom apartment. Only then were we able to buy the "farm of our dreams" and accomplish our other goals. Success takes time. Take the time to create your own success.

Reason #17 – Being Afraid to Try New Things and to Make Mistakes

There are many ways to achieve specific goals. If one marketing strategy does not work, agents often give up without trying other ways to get there. Successful people don't give up. They keep reinventing themselves and how they do things.

Reason #18 — Having Excuses, Excuses, and More Excuses!

I think I have heard all the excuses in the world, always to discover new ones! Here is a small selection of the more memorable excuses, followed by my thoughts (which I did not share with those agents, of course):

"My uncle died... I need to take care of things. I will be back in a month." - I am sorry about your loss, but I know people that have texted with their clients on the way to their parent's funeral. OK, take a day, a week, but a month? And why run away from what you love for so long? Everyone, of course, should do what is best for them. Just thinking to myself...

"I am going to travel in Europe for a while. We will continue when I am back." – I am happy you are finally going to Europe, but Europe is not the moon. I know people that take their laptops and cell phones to other countries all the time, check their emails daily and respond to them. You would not know they are out of town had they not told you. Just thinking to myself again...

"I was in a car accident. I will be fine but need time to recover. I will take a break for a few weeks until I am fully recovered" – I am very sorry. I wish you a quick recovery. Were you hospitalized? Anything broken? "Nothing broken, I drove to urgent care and they sent me home. I will go to a pain specialist and a lawyer later this week". I have been in car accidents myself. Not fun. It can be very painful. But unless you are in an awful condition, maybe you can find some time to work on your laptop in bed? I have done so more than once. Just thinking to myself again...

"I need to take a break while I take some additional real estate courses." – Courses are great!!! But why do you really need a break from something you love so much you want to take more courses about? Just thinking to myself again...

"I tried calling this group of people, but I am not able to convert any of these leads". I provided you these leads one week ago. How many hours did you spend calling them before telling me this is not working for you? Two? Twenty? How about asking me to role play with you again? Just thinking to myself again...

"I joined this networking group one month ago, but I am having no success, so I will stop attending." How many sessions did you attend? – "One". Of course, most of us cannot expect to get people to send us business if we meet them once. Just thinking to myself again...

Step 2 - Sharpening Your Skill Set

Skills Beneficial for Agents and How to Improve on Them!

Let's take a look at the skills agents should ideally possess.

- Ethics
- Assertiveness
- Critical Thinking
- Communication
- Persuasion
- Negotiation
- Time Management
- Project Management

Ethics

Ethics is about having high moral principles that would lead you to strive to do all you can for your actions to result in good for others and no harm to others.

Are you all about making money, or are you concerned with doing the right thing? Are you concerned with protecting your clients and their interests? Doing the right thing for others will, in turn, protect you in this business since they will be less likely to write negative reviews online or file legal actions against you.

If you feel you need to improve on this skill, you could proceed as follows:

1. Learn right and wrong
2. Reflect on what is right and what is wrong
3. Note for yourself what is right and what is wrong
4. Apply your knowledge of what is right and wrong in your daily actions
5. Surround yourself with people that share your values of what is right and what is wrong
6. Lead by example, showing others by doing what is right and refusing to do what is wrong

Assertiveness

Taking control of a situation and doing what needs to be done efficiently is an important quality to possess as an agent. Being assertive is the balance between being passive and aggressive. It encourages two-way communication and exchange and the sharing of opinions and thoughts. Assertiveness promotes cooperation and positive, healthy interpersonal relationships. On the other hand, passive agents are afraid to speak up, not to appear disrespectful, not to upset someone, and just to fit in. You want to be proactive, take charge, especially throughout the escrow/closing process.

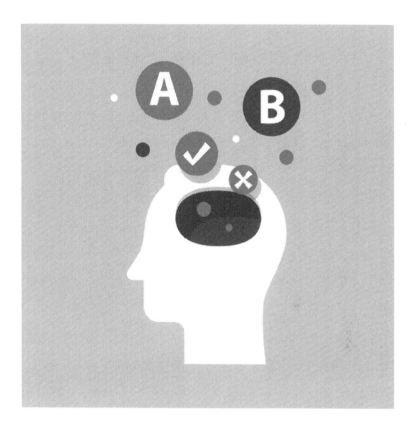

Critical thinking starts with a question, issue, problem, or an opportunity that needs to be handled. Critical thinkers:

1. Look for different ways to handle a situation

2. Evaluate the advantages and disadvantages of each method
3. Select the one that appears to provide the optimal solution
4. Implement the solution
5. Reflect on and learn from the experience

Consider the following example. A seller requests that a property is sold with a tenant inside since the tenant has lived at the property for many years. While the tenant is underpaying rent by a substantial amount, the seller does not wish to evict the tenant due to financial hardship.

Many agents would agree with their clients and proceed as requested. Critical thinkers would look for other ways to handle the situation and see which approach yields the optimal results.

In this example, the agent needs to discuss the situation with the seller. If the agent proceeds as the seller wishes, the property will be sold substantially under market value to an investor. The investor will pay far less since they will calculate that they will need time and money to evict the tenant to bring the property back to profitability. The tenant will lose, and so will the seller. The only winner will be an investor that the seller does not even know.

An agent that is an analytical thinker will explain this to the seller and possibly change the seller's mind.

40

The seller could provide relocation assistance and help the tenant find a new place, and the seller will be able to sell the unit to an owner occupant for a substantially higher price.

Communication

Do you communicate clearly and effectively with those around you? Do you present your clients with your points of view? Or, do you simply follow your client's instructions?

Will you be effective at communicating with the other parties during the transaction? Or, will the buyer's agent walk all over you when they make price reductions and other demands during escrow?

A great communicator is articulate and must also be able to listen actively, which requires undivided attention to understand and resolve conflict and inspire new ideas.

To become a better communicator, you need first to understand the communication process. The communication process consists of a sender, receiver, message, communication channel, and feedback. Communication involves the following steps:

1. Sender defines a message they want to send and a receiver to send the message to.
2. The sender encodes the message
3. The sender selects a communication channel
4. The sender sends a message through the channel
5. The receiver receives the message
6. The receiver decodes the message
7. The receiver provides the sender with feedback

As a sender, your messages need to be well composed, effective, and concise. As a receiver, you need to be able to provide feedback, express your opinions, and explain them.

Persuasion

A good persuader has well developed social skills and can tap into what people think, need, and responds to them accordingly. Persuasion is about being able to match client needs with viable solutions skillfully. Persuasion skills enable you to ask many questions and stay focused on problem solving while keeping the client's needs in mind as a top priority.

You can increase your persuasion abilities by focusing on three things:

- Establishing your own credibility as an expert on the subject matter
- Appealing to your audience's emotions
- Appealing to your audience's logic

Negotiation

Will you sit back and pass your offers from buyers' agents that have unreasonable terms without explaining to your seller why these are unreasonable offers?

Will you pass buyer's requests during escrow for approval without pushing back?

You should be able to see the deal from both sides and make wise business decisions. A negotiation begins with a common goal, such as selling a property. Conflicting interests then arise, most often regarding the price and concessions. A compromise must then be made, meaning some desired goal must be forsaken to achieve the common goal. This involves identifying and resolving all areas of disagreement. Both parties should be willing to budge and give up something tied to their interests and arrive at a final agreement, and you should be comfortable navigating these waters.

Time Management

There is so much that agents can do. Marketing is only limited by the imagination. So, you will need time. And, given the limited time we all have in our busy lives, time management is critical to create success.

There are different ways to look at time management. A common approach includes the following steps:

- Make a list of the activities you need to handle. Add to this list as new activities arise.
- Define a deadline and a priority level for each activity.
- Each time you revisit your list, sort it by priority level and deadlines

- Attempt to complete the task at the top of your list
- If a higher priority task arrives with a short deadline, you may consider taking a break from the task you are working on and proceeding to work on this new task. Later you can go back to the task you were working on before you were interrupted.
- Once you are done with a task, pick the next task on your list to work on, and if needed, re-order the list first.

This can be done with a simple spreadsheet or a CRM application. I have come to conclude that for me, a simple spreadsheet is... simply simpler!

Project Management

Life may appear complicated, and even more so once you start in real estate. It does not need to be so. One way to simplify life, including the real estate related aspects of it, is to divide almost everything you do into more manageable projects. A project is defined by the Project Management Institute (PMI – www.pmi.org) as a temporary endeavor that has a defined beginning and end, scope, and resources. For example, you can treat a specific marketing campaign to reach a particular group of people as a project. You could treat writing an article about what you do for a blog as a project, and so on.

You can also define smaller projects within larger projects. Once a project is defined, you can add it to your list of tasks/projects discussed in the previous section in this book and treat it according to its priority. This strategy breaks down life in general and your real estate efforts in particular into more manageable components!

Proven project management skills are very beneficial to closing real estate deals. The PMI defines five phases to project management. These include project initiation, planning, execution, monitoring/controlling, and closing. There are also ten knowledge areas to manage. They include integration, scope, time, cost, quality, human resources, communication, risk, procurement, and stakeholder management.

Step 3 - Defining Your Focus

The Focus Areas of Real Estate Agents

A Real Estate Agent career is the most common real estate career people pursue. Real estate agents help people sell or buy properties. You can be a buyers' agent representing buyers or a listing agent representing sellers, or both. You can also be either a residential agent, a commercial agent or both. Finally, you can be a leasing agent representing landlords, tenants, or both. You will need a real estate license to practice as a real estate agent in most states.

Residential Real Estate Agent

Residential real estate agents facilitate the home buying process between sellers and buyers. To be successful, you need an effective marketing strategy that generates leads and a lead conversion strategy. Real estate is mostly marketing, so you need to enjoy doing that. You also need to provide excellent service to your clients. Excellent service results in positive reviews online, client referrals, and repeat business.

You can also typically take various courses at your local association of realtors and become certified in any of several specialties.

Some agents handle all residential properties, while others specialize in one or more specific property types:

- Single-family homes
- Condominiums (Condos)
- Luxury homes
- Vacation homes
- Foreclosures/REOs
- Probate properties

Your state association of realtors may offer a variety of certifications, such as:

- First-time buyer specialist
- Investment property specialist
- Probate and trust specialist
- Buyer's representative
- International property specialist
- Military relocation professional
- Resort and second home specialist
- Senior real estate specialist
- Short sale and foreclosure specialist

Listing Agents focus on representing sellers. **Buyers Agents** focus on representing buyers. Many agents act as both listing and buyers' agents.

Representing sellers typically requires developing deep relations with people until months or years later, your growing reputation starts to bring sellers knocking on your door. In this role, you will price properties, market properties, review offers, negotiate with buyers' agents, and manage the escrow process to close. You may also need to oversee evictions, cash for keys, property preservation, renovation, and maintenance in certain situations (see Step 8).

Representing buyers involves deep relations as well. In this role, you will present buyers with properties that match their criteria, show those properties they are interested in, help determine what price and terms to offer for the property they would like to purchase, write offers, negotiate terms, and manage the escrow process to close.

Commercial Real Estate Agent

Commercial real estate agents handle the acquisition and/or disposition of commercial real estate assets. Types of commercial real estate include multi-family (5+ units), retail, industrial, office, land, shopping centers, hospitality, flex, healthcare, sports and entertainment, student housing, etc. As in residential real estate, marketing and excellent service are essential. Commercial agents work with data like capitalization rates (CAP), gross rent multipliers (GRM), and internal rates of return (IRR). Therefore, you need to like to work with numbers to perform analysis, and having some business and financial knowledge is also beneficial.

Commercial real estate agents help businesses find locations that fit their needs. They help individuals and companies that wish to invest in commercial real estate assets identify, negotiate, and purchase such assets.

Commercial agents often must uncover statistics and data about the area before they commence a transaction.

Residential Leasing Agent

Residential leasing agents work with property owners/landlords to find suitable tenants to lease their rental properties to. Other leasing agents work with tenants or both owners and tenants. You can focus on leasing luxury homes or apartments in a specific area, for example.

Commercial Leasing Agent

Commercial leasing agents work with property owners/landlords to find suitable tenants to lease their commercial properties to. These agents may handle leasing of any type of commercial assets or focus on one or more: multi-family (5+ units), retail, industrial, office, land, shopping centers, hospitality, flex, healthcare, sports and entertainment, student housing, and others. You can represent landlords (Landlord Rep), represent tenants (Tenant Rep), or both. You will need to become familiar with the characteristics of commercial properties, as well as with the needs of tenants and work to match them. You will then engage in negotiations of terms and execution of contracts, which may include overseeing tenant improvements.

Step 4 - Choosing Your Brokerage

Once you pass your real estate salesperson's state exam and receive your license, it is time to find a broker to hang your license with.

Real estate sales and leasing is a business of relationships. Relationships with clients, lenders, relationships with fellow agents, and with many others. In most cases, an essential relation you can have when getting started is with your broker. An experienced and caring broker can be valuable in helping you become successful.

It's important to schedule calls with multiple brokerages to see if you are a good fit for them, and they are a good fit for you. You should be interviewing each other. Most brokerages are continuously looking for agents and will be happy to speak with you.

If you have not taken your exam yet, schedule interviews anyway. You can learn about various opportunities before you get your license and be ready to join the brokerage that is right for you as soon as you receive your license.

Choosing the right brokerage is critical to your success. The 13 key factors involved in making the right decision for you are:

- Commission
- Fees
- Training
- Mentoring
- Management support
- Administrative support
- Brokerage focus area(s)
- Referrals and leads
- Internet presence
- Culture
- Brokerage size
- Facilities
- Location

The following is a look at each of these 13 key factors in more detail.

The vast majority of agents get paid commission only. The commission is paid once a deal is closed and the property is either sold or leased. Different brokers offer different commission splits to their agents. Commissions can be negotiated in many cases as you gain more experience in the industry.

Here in Los Angeles, for example, a typical commission is 5%. If you sell a $700,000 property, the total commission is 5% of this amount. It is usually split equally between the listing agent and the buyer's agent. If you represent one side, 2.5% is 17,500. A portion of this commission goes to your broker, so if you have a 60-40 split with your broker, you get to keep 60% of 17,500, which is $10,500. Remember that you need to pay taxes on this amount but can also deduct certain expenses as an independent contractor.

What is a reasonable commission split? The answer to that depends on the following:

- Which area of the country you live in, and what standards are there
- What level of support the broker provides

- How motivated the broker is to have you join their brokerage as an agent

The key is to understand what you will be receiving, given the split offered. The split should not be your primary consideration when selecting a brokerage to start your career.

If a broker can help get your business off the ground, they should receive a reasonable portion of the commission. Remember, 100% of nothing is nothing, so why worry about the split when getting started?

Many brokerages start new agents at a 60-40% split. In these cases, most of the overhead expenses are paid by the real estate company.

Some brokers offer 100% commission. Note that they will make you pay in other ways, with transaction fees, Errors and Omissions (E&O) insurance premiums, and desk fees, and they will probably offer you very little or no assistance.

Join the brokerage you like the most, do not focus on negotiating commission and other terms. You can and should do that later once you learn the business and start to consistently close deals.

Many brokerages charge fees. Fees may include any combination of the following:

- Transaction fees
- Desk fees

- Technology Fees
- Print fees
- Copy fees
- Insurance fees

Add up all the fees to determine your monthly, annual, and/or per-transaction costs. Ask yourself this: why should any brokerage charge you any monthly or annual fees? Are they in the business of collecting fees or in the business of helping their agents close deals to everyone's benefit?

Training

Preparing for the state exam does not prepare you for creating a successful business for yourself in the real world. Now that you have a license, you need to learn many topics, including but not limited to the following:

- Determining property values based on comparables. Creating BPO reports for clients
- Filling out real estate forms and contracts for a variety of situations
- What marketing works and what is not likely to work, and why
- Communication strategies

- Negotiation strategies

Essential questions you should find answers to:

- Who will be training you?
- What is their practical experience?
- What is their training experience?
- How long have they been in real estate?
- What is their real estate experience?
- How long have they been training?
- What is the format of the training?
- How much time do they have for you?

Ongoing training is vital for any agent, given how fast technology is changing the business, regardless of how long they have been in the industry.

If a brokerage offers classes, ask to sit on one of the classes and see if you would benefit from the experience before joining the brokerage if this is your primary selection consideration. If a brokerage claims to be providing one-on-one training, ask to experience a conversation with your trainer to be, perhaps via zoom.

Mentoring

You will likely need, as most new agents do, someone to mentor you. That person should guide you at each step of your first few deals.

Your mentor will be crucial to your success. You should schedule a virtual meeting with the person who will be your mentor before deciding to join a specific brokerage. You should determine:

- How available will they be
- What their plan is
- What their compensation is for mentoring you
- If you see yourself spending time with them and learning from them.

Good mentors should love mentoring. It should be in their personality. This should be much more than about the money. You will need to see if they have the right personality for the role and for you given your own personality.

Management Support

On many occasions, you need access to the broker/owner. Having a mentor is great, but if the mentor is not the broker/owner, you also need access to the broker or another decision-maker in the brokerage. You need to identify who they will be and see if they have enough time available to help you.

If a broker/owner also works on their own deals, they may be too busy to help you, so there should be someone else in a decision-making capacity that has the time to help you.

One person in a management capacity is usually not able to effectively oversee more than 40-50 agents, so if you are joining a brokerage with hundreds of agents, make sure there is a team of decision-makers available to help those agents so that you can get timely responses.

Administrative Support

Many agents are attracted to offices that provide support with paperwork. There is someone that can load the property on the MLS for you, someone to write your offers and handle your escrows. Sounds great, but this is not the way to learn the business. To know the business, you need to understand and experience each step of the process, and the process is a bit different each time you go through it. Therefore, you should do it all yourself (with your mentor's help) for the first few times. At that stage, one of two things will happen. You might realize that you want to keep doing it now that you know how to do it, or you might want to pass it on to someone else.

A brokerage may provide you an in-house person to handle your paperwork (and there is usually a cost to that, such as a specific fee or a lower split for you), or you can find endless independent transaction coordinators yourself to work with.

Brokerage Focus Area(s)

Many brokerages focus strictly on residential real estate. Some brokerages focus strictly on commercial real estate. Others handle both residential and commercial transactions.

Some residential brokerages further specialize in one or more of these areas:

- Working with seniors
- Working with investors
- Working with first time home buyers
- Working with condo owners
- Residential Leasing
- Vacation homes
- Luxury Sales
- Luxury Leasing
- Bank owned properties (REO)
- Probate properties

Commercial brokerages focus on sales, leasing, property management, or a combination of. They may further focus on one or more of the following types of commercial real estate:

- Multi-family (5+ units)
- Retail
- Industrial
- Office
- Land
- Shopping centers
- Hospitality
- Flex

- Healthcare
- Sports and entertainment
- Student housing
- Specialty (other)

Some brokerages will let you work in multiple specialization areas. Other brokerages have strict guidelines on what the office handles.

Leads and Referrals

For significant long-term success, you eventually need to be able to generate your own leads. Until then, it can be of benefit to you if the brokerage provides you with leads once in a while.

Brokerages get inquiries to their website, and people call in on specific properties for sale without a particular agent in mind.

Find out who gets those leads and how it is decided. Some brokerages send them to experienced agents that are known to close deals. Other brokerages send them to the new agents to help them get started on their careers.

Learn the potential cost of leads provided by the brokerage, and remember, there is usually no free lunch.

Internet Presence

Most people use the internet and will check you and your brokerage out online. Your broker's website should be professional and up to date.

The brokerage website should be promoting the brand, the brokerage, and its agents.

Culture

At the end of the day, unless you partner with any other agents in the office and share commission, they are your competition, and you should carefully evaluate and triple-check their advice before you take it.

Are you looking for a boutique brokerage with an intimate, family-like brokerage culture? Or do you prefer a national or regional franchise brokerage where you will likely need to be on guard? Are you looking for get-togethers and brokerage caravans on open house day?

Remember, other agents are, for the most part, your competition. Are you looking to socialize with your competition? Will they teach you what you need to know or direct you into paths on which you will spin your wheels and burn your tires?

If you love your independence and do not like corporate culture, an independent brokerage may be the way to go. The main advantage of joining a franchise is name recognition, but then the market is saturated with these names.

No matter what culture you choose, you need to enjoy being in it, which will motivate you to continue on the path.

Brokerage Size

There are advantages and disadvantages to joining large or small brokerages.

Advantages of Large Brokerages:

- You might like the energy of a large office.
- Training classes for agents may be offered.
- Brand name recognition.

Disadvantages of Large Brokerages:

- Plenty of motivational meetings that waste time and provide little benefit otherwise.
- Rigid procedures may not work for you.
- Leads coming to the brokerage likely will go to those agents that are closer to the broker.
- Not likely to accommodate new ideas.
- Their strategy is to bring in as many agents as possible and see who sticks within their environment, not to accommodate and ensure each agent's success.

Advantages of Small Brokerages:

- The cohesiveness of a smaller office environment.
- One on one mentoring and coaching for agents.
- Local brand name recognition.
- It is in their interest to make sure whoever they bring on is successful, as they do not have the time or resources to bring in masses of new agents.
- You will be working directly with the broker or a person assigned by them.
- Fewer leads will come to the brokerage, but you will have a better shot at those leads when they come in because fewer agents are around.

- Much more flexibility to discuss and implement creative ideas to grow your own business within the brokerage.

Disadvantages of Small Brokerages:

- Likely no classroom-type training
- Lack of name recognition of a big brand.

Facilities

Clients do not go into offices much, if at all, these days. They expect you to come to them, meet them at properties, and for the most part, communicate with them electronically.

If you insist on joining a brokerage with an office, consider the following:

- The look of the office
- Reasonable workspace size for you
- Use of computer and copier
- After-hours access to the office
- Parking availability and cost

In the world of Zoom, many would say there is no longer a need to go to the office. The time to drive, the cost of gas, wear and tear of the car, parking cost, and dry cleaning is unnecessary.

Meetings can be more effective via zoom, transaction management software allows you to eliminate the need for paperwork, mail can be sent to your home, and networking with other agents can be done via zoom. So why have an office? How often will you go there? For what reasons?

Step 5 - Defining Your Unique Selling Proposition

A Unique Selling Proposition (USP) is something, possibly a benefit, that makes you and your real estate business stand out when compared to other real estate agents in your market.

You need to identify what makes your real estate business unique, given so much competition all around, to target your sales efforts successfully. What will you specialize in? What will your focus be? Let us look at some options to choose from.

International Buyers Specialist

It would help if you learned about what buyers from one or more countries are looking to purchase in terms of

US vacation homes, US residential investment properties, or commercial investment properties. You should offer them full services, including zoom meetings and virtual tours. You help them arrange flights, accommodations, transportation, and entertainment while visiting to view properties in-person. You help with all the usual aspects of buyer representation, connect them with attorneys and CPAs that specialize in international investors. You also help with property management once the deal is done.

Commercial Off Market Specialist

You need to get to know a select group of commercial real estate owners and be on top of who wants to buy what and who wants to sell what. You get paid for introducing deals to buyers before they hit the market.

Why off market? Many commercial owners do not wish to list properties for sale on the market. That is, they do not want to list them on the local MLS, LoopNet, or Costar. Why? In many situations, the owners do not wish for the tenants to become aware the property is for sale so that the tenant(s) do not start worrying about having a new landlord that may make changes such as wish to increase their rent. Why? Since worried tenants are more likely to start looking for a new place to lease. Fewer tenants mean reduced values of the assets.

First Time Home Buyers Specialist

You need to learn how to build trust with first time home buyers and make them your customers for life. You need to be able to deliver information to them on available mortgage programs to help them overcome the financing obstacles they may be experiencing and turn their challenges into opportunities.

You need to understand the issues facing today's first-time homebuyers in order to offer them the highest level of service. Buyer's families often get involved in the buying process, so you need to learn how to handle them.

First time home buyers are often unsure which area(s) they can afford to live in, so you will need to educate them on the pricing and other characteristics of different neighborhoods in their price range.

As part of being a first-time buyers specialist, you might want to prepare appropriate materials and create and run first-time buyer workshops. You will need to learn to educate and guide first-time buyers through the home buying process.

Down Payment / Closing Costs Assistance Programs Specialist

You need to learn about products and resources that can help modest-income borrowers buy homes of their own. These include down payment assistance programs as well as closing costs assistance programs. You will then educate modest-income borrowers about these programs, introduce them to these programs and help them apply for such assistance.

You would then proceed to help these buyers find the right homes and purchase them.

Senior Real Estate Specialist

You need to build skills in selling the family home and moving to an active-adult community. It would help if you also learned how to counsel seniors and develop and maintain relations with them. You will need to understand the types of housing available for the senior market. You will need to learn how reverse mortgages, pensions, 401(k) accounts, and IRAs impact real estate decisions, help clients integrate disposition of real property into estate plans, ensure you comply with federal laws, including the Housing for Older Persons Act (HOPA), Assemble a team of experts to help you serve senior clients and customers.

Vacation Homes Specialist

Your buyers' interests will range from small, country getaways to luxury properties. You clients will likely include international and local clients wishing to purchase investments or for their own use.

You can also represent sellers and manage properties in vacation destinations. You will need to understand these markets. It would be beneficial for you to understand the tax implications of such investments and have a CPA and attorney on your extended team.

You need to build up your skills that will allow buyers and sellers to have confidence in your ability to help them buy, sell or manage vacation properties for investment, development, or retirement. You will need to build expertise in second homes in a resort, recreational, and/or vacation destination(s).

Foreclosed Properties (REO) Specialist

You need to know how to perform detailed pricing analysis and create detailed custom reports.

You also need to know how to work with lawyers on cash for keys offers and evictions procedures. You may need to attend court to represent the seller during evictions. You need to know how to work with vendors and oversee their work as they preserve and/or enhance properties' physical condition.

You need to know how to handle multiple offer situations that are very common in this business and manage the extra, REO-specific steps during the offer processing and escrow management portions of the transactions.

Short Sales Specialist

A short sale is usually a situation where the property is worth less than the mortgage that is owed. The seller likely has a hardship situation that is preventing them from keeping the property.

A typical workflow starts when the property is listed on the MLS, indicating the sale will be contingent on lender approval. The lender is presented with an offer, accepted by the seller, along with a completed short sale package and an explanation elucidating why the short sale is necessary.

If the lender approves the offer, escrow can close as usual, and all proceeds go to the lender.

You will need to understand how to direct distressed sellers to finance, tax, and legal professionals. You will also need to know how to qualify sellers for short sales, develop a short sale package, negotiate with lenders while protecting the buyers and your commission.

Probate Sales Specialist

This discussion is based on the California Probate Code and may be different in your state.

The Probate Real Estate Sales Specialist focuses on selling properties that are part of a probate petition. The administrator or executor is issued either limited or full authority to sell the real estate by the judge. A Probate Real Estate Sales Specialist understands the probate process and forms required and can protect the best interest of the heirs of the estate.

With limited authority probate, the sale requires court confirmation and must adhere to specific probate codes. The property must sell for at least 90% of the probate referee's appraised value. The court must approve the sale, and this provides an opportunity for overbidding in court. The Probate Real Estate Sales Specialist continues to market the property once an offer is accepted, subject to court confirmation.

The accepted offer must have no contingencies, and the deposit amount must be 10% of the purchase price, delivered to the administrator or executor upon offer acceptance. The goal is to bring as many buyers as possible to the court hearing for overbidding and drive the price up as high as possible.

The specialist must meet with the buyers who come to the court hearing at the courthouse and vet them to ensure they are qualified to bid. They must have a cashier's check in the amount of 10% of the initial overbid price as well as proof of funds for the entire purchase price. The qualified buyers will be allowed to participate in the overbid process at the court hearing. The winning bidder will sign a court order prepared by the probate attorney at the court hearing, which is provided to escrow.

In a full authority sale, the administrator or executor has the authority to sell the property without court confirmation and without having to adhere to probate codes. An offer is accepted with terms that the administrator or executor feels comfortable with, at which time a Notice of Proposed Action is issued by the probate attorney to the heirs notifying them of the terms of the proposed sale. If within 15 days there is no objection to the sale, escrow proceeds with closing. If there are any objections, the sale becomes one that requires court confirmation.

Step 6 - Defining Your Target Market

It is not practical for most new agents to effectively target a large part of the market. It is best to focus on a few thousand people in a narrower market segment. Some of the possible market segments for you to consider are discussed next.

Single Family Homeowners

You can target all homeowners in specific zip codes/areas. You can target homeowners by narrowing the criteria to include homes over or under a specific interior square footage or homes under or over a specific estimated value.

Condo Owners

You can focus on condo owners in specific zip codes or areas, interior square footage limits, or condo values. You can further narrow your focus to particular buildings and complexes.

Investors

You can focus on building relationships with investors. Investors love deals and sometimes want to sell their properties, so this is a source of buyers and sellers.

You can find active investors in commercial databases such as CoStar.com by searching for those that have recently purchased certain types of assets. For example, you can choose to focus on all individuals and entities that own three or more single-family homes in your area. If you want larger fish, focus on those that own ten or more single-family homes and so forth.

Professionals

People who practice in certain professions are more likely to generate more income and invest in real estate themselves, and be associated in private and/or business to others that also invest in real estate.

These professionals include attorneys, medical doctors, certified public accountants, and others.

High Net Worth Individuals

You can focus on individuals attending certain country clubs, tennis clubs, golf clubs, as well as other clubs and organizations in your area. You can attempt to join these organizations.

You can meet such individuals by joining the boards of non-profit organizations and/or attending events that are attended by high net worth individuals. Such strategies, of course, require your financial investment.

Commercial Asset Owners

You can focus on owners of commercial real estate. Commercial asset owners primarily own multi-family (5+ units), retail, industrial, office, land, shopping centers, hospitality, flex, healthcare, sports and entertainment, and/or student housing.

You can find them and their contact information in databases such as CoStar.com

You can reach out to them to see if there is anything they wish to sell off-market and then present the deals to other commercial asset owners in your network.

Institutional Owners, Servicers, and Asset Management Companies

Real Estate Owned (REO) assets are assets that did not sell successfully at a foreclosure auction and are now owned by the lender.

You can approach financial institutions such as Wells Fargo, Bank of America, and many other national, state, or local banks as well as non-bank entities to help them dispose of their REOs. You can also approach asset management companies and servicers and offer them to do the same thing.

Please note that these organizations have complex disposition procedures that are very labor-intensive for the agents that help them dispose of their REO assets. You will need to become an expert at creating broker price opinions as well as monthly status reports. You will need to visit properties weekly, take detailed interior and exterior photos, and provide them to these corporate clients via their online portals. Such work is best suited for type A personalities that have assistants and contractors to support them!

You will need to oversee cash for keys negotiations, evictions, property preservation, and renovation efforts on behalf of your clients.

Age Groups

You can target a particular age group in your area.

The Silent Generation was born in 1945 and before. Baby boomers were born between 1946 and 1964, Gen X was born between 1965 and 1980, and Gen Y, or Millennials, were born between 1981 and 1996.

You can target one or more of these groups based on your comfort level or expertise related to a specific age range (For example, you might be a nursing care provider in your other career to members of the Silent Generation).

Ethnic / Religious Groups

You can target your own ethnic or religious group or any other group if you like. You can target anyone in such a group or further focus on high-net-worth individuals, professionals, and or business owners in your target group.

90

Business Owners

You can approach and build relationships with business owners that may be able to send you referrals. For example, you can target wedding planners to refer to you newlyweds looking for their first homes.

Location

You can target individuals or organizations in specific zip codes or areas. You can get data from your title company and append phone and email information through other data providers. You have to make sure you operate within applicable laws, of course, when emailing or calling prospects.

Step 7 - Marketing Yourself, Your Brand, and Your Services

I have seen intelligent people fail, and many others that are not so brilliant create great success. Success in real estate is not about intelligence as it is about being more popular and more liked than your competition.

How do you go about gaining popularity? By marketing your magnificent personality, your fabulous brand, and the services you provide (which, of course, exceed all expectations!).

It's Much About Marketing!

Most people that start a real estate sales career fail within one to two years. It takes time to create success in real estate. Some get lucky and close a deal within the first few months, but for many others, it may take 1-2 years or more to start generating income consistently and longer in commercial real estate.

What distinguishes many of those that do succeed from the majority that does not is their ability to stay focused and not give up. It also helps to have some money saved and/or a part or even full-time job. You will need money to live and money to invest in your business.

Investing money in your business can be in the form of joining a local board of realtors and the local multiple listing service. You should also be able to invest some money in marketing yourself, your brand, and your services.

To market yourself, you need to define what you specialize in, to clearly define your unique selling point (USP), and your target market segment. You need to exude trust and credibility!

The following is an overview to give you a flavor of what much of your career will be about: marketing yourself, your brand, and your services. It is not the goal of this step to provide an in-depth, comprehensive treatment of this topic. Many books have been written on real estate marketing.

Your Digital Footprint

People search for you before they meet you and after they meet you. Search yourself online and see what they will see.

They should be able to find the following about you, your brand, and your services:

- Your website
- You on your broker's website
- Your LinkedIn profile
- Your other social media profiles
- Photos of you
- Videos of you
- Articles you wrote
- Articles written about you

Website

Your website should be focused on conveying your USP to your target audience.

Your website would include:

- Information about you
- Information about your services
- Your videos
- Articles you wrote or that were written about you
- Your or your broker's listings
- MLS search for all listings in the market

- News
- Contact us page

Videos

People love watching videos! You should focus on creating the following types of videos:

- Showcasing your real estate listings (or those of your broker)
- Discussing who you are and your services
- Discussing various real estate topics
- Discussing social topics you care about
- Interviewing other professionals related to your business
- Showcasing streets, neighborhoods, and businesses
- Showcasing community events

If you are short on funds, you can shoot videos yourself, have a family member or friend shoot them, or find a college student specializing in a related field to help you and gain experience in the process.

Once you create each video, upload it to YouTube, insert the YouTube link into your website and post it on social media.

Your Existing Network

It takes time to develop relations before converting them to sales (first to prospects and then prospects to customers). An excellent place to start for many agents is their existing personal and/or professional network. It can include the following categories of people you already know:

- Family contacts
- Friends
- Neighbors
- K-12 Classmates
- College/University contacts
- Colleagues from previous places of work
- Contacts from the places of worship you attend/attended
- Contacts from social/sports clubs you attend/attended
- Facebook and other social media friends (that are not in any of the above categories)

You might want to spend some time collecting these contacts into a spreadsheet or a CRM application.

Marketing to Your Existing Network

Let everyone in your existing network know that you became a real estate agent and that you are happy to help them. Ask them if you can help them at this time. If they do not require your services now, ask when you should check in with them again about this.

You can do this via email, text, and/or phone or zoom conversations.

Did I mention you need to exude trust and credibility?

Referrals from Your Existing Network

At a certain stage, you should ask every person you know for a referral to other people that may need your services or that could help you grow your business.

Expanding your Network

Some new agents start their careers with a fantastic existing network and do not have a great urgency to add to this network. For most agents, however, this is not the case. Most agents are not able to significantly capitalize on their existing network. They need to expand it to the target market segment(s) they decided to pursue (as discussed earlier in this book).

Marketing is key to your success as a real estate agent, and marketing never ends. Think of major brands in any industry. They continuously market their products and services. You will need to do the same.

Marketing to your Expanding Network

You will need to work on defining and implementing your custom marketing campaigns. They will be based on your USP and directed to your target market segment(s).

You will need to select various marketing channels, define specific campaigns for each channel, measure each campaign's effectiveness, and then adjust your future campaigns based on lessons learned.

A good broker should help you with your marketing strategy to get you going.

Marketing Channels

There are traditional marketing channels as well as online marketing channels you can select from. Experimentation will show you which ones work best for you.

Traditional marketing channels include:

- Advertising in paper publications
- Writing articles for paper publications
- Bench advertising
- Mailing flyers to peoples' homes
- Calling people, keeping in mind the National Do Not Call Registry
- Joining organizations, attending meetings, events
- Create events either yourself or as part of the organizations you are involved in

Online marketing channels include (keep in mind applicable laws):

- Mass email
- Mass text
- Mass voice mails
- LinkedIn and other social media – to connect, communicate and post messages
- Blogging

What Next?

Ultimately you must speak with people on the phone, zoom with them, and of course, meet with them to convert them to sellers and/or buyers and grow your pipeline of real estate business.

Some leads from your marketing efforts are ready to make a move and sell, purchase, lease at this time, others may require a follow-up campaign to turn them from cold leads to warm leads, and finally to paying customers.

Step 8 - Executing Transactions to Near Perfection

Introduction

Executing a real estate transaction as flawlessly as possible will increase your chances of both repeat business and referrals. This step looks at what successful real estate agents do, from establishing property values to closing deals. Major phases include valuation (pricing) of real estate, and handling occupied properties before listing for sale, handling vacant properties including property preservation and renovation, marketing properties, managing offers, and closings (escrow).

Near flawless execution will help you exude more trust and credibility!

Property Valuation

You need to be able to establish a realistic value of a real estate asset you are handling. A property's value is a critical factor in establishing a property's list price prior to disposition. It is also important to establish value when helping with real estate acquisition to determine what maximum amount it makes sense to pay for properties.

You need to be able to create Broker Price Opinion (BPO) reports for residential properties and Broker Opinion of Value (BOV) reports for commercial properties. You then need to learn to establish list prices for residential and commercial properties based on these reports.

Handling Occupied Properties

Most of the time, you will be selling properties that are either vacant or have paying tenants that are generating income for the properties.

From time to time, issues arise with occupied properties. These include illegal units, rent control, tenants not paying rent, tenants preventing access, and more.

You need to know how to handle the disposition of occupied properties in situations where the occupants' presence reduces the likely sale price substantially.

You need to understand strategies for handling occupied properties, including relocation assistance, the eviction process, and the handling of abandoned personal property after termination of occupancy.

Handling Vacant Properties

You need to ensure properties you are handling are secure. You should help secure them if they are not. A decision needs to be made if to sell the property as-is or renovate it. Actions need to be taken to preserve the condition of the property. Hazards and vandalism need to be handled if encountered.

Property preservation activities are undertaken to preserve the current condition of a property. They include:

- Rekey
- Handling HOA requirements
- Handling state/local requirements
- Requesting Pre-Sale Report
- Organizing personal property and disposing of it
- Trash Out – removal of trash from the property
- Emergency services
- Sales clean
- Carpet shampoo
- Yard maintenance
- Pool maintenance
- General repairs
- Termite repairs
- Specialized repairs

You may also offer to help oversee a minor or major renovation of a property before its sale, thus increasing the value you provide to your customers.

You need to become an expert at marketing the properties you list for sale or lease. These marketing activities include:

- Signage – residential signs, commercial signs, open house signs
- Professional photos of properties
- Professionally composed property descriptions
- Professional video and 3D virtual tour
- Professional websites for properties
- Placing properties on the MLS for residential and small commercial properties, and on LoopNet and CoStar for all commercial properties
- Traditional Marketing – placing ads showcasing the properties in local papers and magazines
- Electronic Marketing – includes emailing a flyer of the property to agents and buyers, texting about the property to agents and/or buyers, posting ads of the property in your social media accounts, advertising the property for sale on various websites such as apartments.com.
- Conducting open houses
- Showing properties

- Handling price reductions

Managing Offers

You need to know how to write offers for your buyer clients and how to handle incoming offers for the purchase of your listings. You need to become familiar with the basic components of an offer package, including the state purchase contract, proof of funds, pre-approval letter, and additional components that apply depending on the situation.

You need to learn to present offers to sellers, help them select offers, count offers, and employ different negotiation strategies.

You also need to gain experience assembling the contract package, getting it signed by the parties to the contract, and distributing it.

When representing sellers, you need to become an expert in:

- Receiving offers from buyers and/or their agents

- Understanding the basic components of a complete offer package
- Reviewing State Purchase Contract/Purchase Agreements and identifying errors or missing items.
- Reviewing Proof of Funds (POF)
- Reviewing Loan Pre-Approval Letters (PAL)
- Understanding the additional components of a complete offer package and when they apply and making sure they were provided
- Presenting offers to sellers
- Fully disclosing everything known about the property to potential buyers
- Selecting offers
- Countering offers
- Knowing when to use a Counter and when to use an Addendum
- Receiving, reviewing, and executing the Contract Package

When representing buyers, you need to become an expert at:

- Creating offers for properties on behalf of your buyers

- Understanding the basic components of a complete offer package
- Reviewing State Purchase Contract/Purchase Agreements
- Reviewing Proof of Funds (POF) and making sure they are appropriate before submitting to listing agents
- Reviewing Loan Pre-Approval Letters (PAL) before submitting to listing agents
- Understanding the additional components of a complete offer package and when they apply and making sure they are provided
- Sending offers to listing agents
- Responding to counter offers
- Knowing when to use a Counter and when to use an Addendum
- Assembling the Contract Package
- Receiving, reviewing, and executing the Contract Package
- Sending the Fully Executed Contract to the listing agent

Managing the Escrow Process

You should gain experience in the numerous activities that occur from the time an escrow company is notified to open escrow and assigns an escrow number to the time when the keys are turned in to the buyer and money to the seller (and you get paid, of course!).

As I defined in my book "The Practical Guide to Career Opportunities in Real Estate: A Survey of Over 35 Careers with a Focus on Becoming an Excellent Real Estate Agent", the escrow process is divided into five phases. The first phase includes activities to perform just before opening escrow, followed by initial escrow period activities, activities throughout escrow, activities during the final part of escrow, and activities immediately once escrow closes.

You need to be able to execute the five-phase escrow process to a successful conclusion.

Period Activities (Phase 1):

- Preliminary title report due diligence
- Research and handle city pre-sale requirements
- Compile seller's disclosure package
- Confirm utilities on/turn on utilities
- Order products and services

Initial Escrow Period Activities (Phase 2):

- Set MLS status to Pending
- Send "Request to Open Escrow" email

Intermediate Escrow Period Activities (Phase 3):

- Confirm that escrow received buyer's deposit
- Ensure contingencies are removed
- Repairs required to be made during escrow
- Order home warranty plan

Activities at End of Escrow Period (Phase 4):

These are typically handled one week prior to closing.

- Contact lender to determine closing readiness

- Determine escrow office readiness
- Contact buyer's agent to determine closing readiness
- Final verification of property condition

Pending to Sold Activities (Phase 5)

- Reminder to turn off utilities
- Request lawn/pool services be terminated
- Remove sign
- Set MLS status to Sold

Managing Client Expectations and Relations

Whether you represent buyers, sellers, landlords, or tenants, it is critical to manage their expectations and proactively and positively control your relations with them.

Your clients might be new to real estate, have extensive experience with real estate, or anything in between. You should quickly determine their level of real estate experience and adjust your strategy with them accordingly.

You need to exude confidence and establish yourself as their trusted advisor. It is my hope that this book started you on this path!

If you have any ideas for improvement of this book, please email me at david@GeffenRealEstate.com or text me at 310-433-0694

If you enjoyed this book, please consider posting a review. Even if it's only a few sentences, it would be a huge help. Thank you.

Made in the USA
Las Vegas, NV
30 March 2023

69925769R00066